ECK Wisdom *on* Solving Problems

ECK WISDOM

on

Solving Problems

HAROLD KLEMP

ECKANKAR
Minneapolis
www.Eckankar.org

ECK Wisdom on Solving Problems

 161107

Printed in USA

Photo of Sri Harold Klemp (page 94)
by Art Galbraith

Library of Congress Cataloging-in-Publication Data

Names: Klemp, Harold, author.
Title: ECK wisdom on solving problems / Harold Klemp.
Description: Minneapolis : Eckankar, 2017.
Identifiers: LCCN 2017002152 | ISBN 9781570434464
(pbk. : alk. paper)
Subjects: LCSH: Eckankar (Organization) | Problem-solving--Religious aspects--Eckankar (Organization)
Classification: LCC BP605.E3 K55387 2017 | DDC 299/.93--dc23
LC record available at https://lccn.loc.gov/2017002152

∞ This paper meets the requirements of ANSI/NISO Z39.48-1992 (Permanence of Paper).

Contents

It's Your Story—You're the Star

Sometimes your life seems to flow like a well-written script. You can handle the story line. If a problem arises, you can solve it by yourself.

It's your story, you're the star, everything's going great, and the world loves you.

Then you come to a chapter that seems to have been devised by a very poor scriptwriter. Problems come up with your health, personal relationships, job, finances, or anything of this nature. All of a sudden, you can't handle it. This is when you say, "Help!"

There is nothing wrong with asking for help, but we must remember that our purpose for being on earth is to learn how to arrive at the correct solution to our own problems. We have to write the script and—as well as we can—figure out how to untangle the plot.

If we can't get ourselves out of the fix, there is always *deus ex machina*. This is divine intervention and is a true, spiritual quality of the teachings of ECK. It is the essential element.

An equally essential part of the teachings is to develop your creativity. Then you can learn to resolve your own problems. These are problems that you have made for yourself. Out of the factors that made these problems, surely there must be solutions.

Grinding of Life

What kinds of problems? Usually we talk about problems in a spiritual sense—something big such as a lack of faith, fear of life, fear of death, or no love.

And when we speak of these lofty problems, those on the grand scale, we often overlook the problems of daily living.

The problems we most often encounter in life are ones like buying a new pair of shoes before the cracks in the old pair begin to look like very stylized leather.

Or we run into health problems, problems on the job, problems in a relationship, or problems with losing the love of someone who is very dear to us. These are the everyday things that grind the human consciousness down into a piece of gravel and then into sand.

And out of this constant grinding of life we suddenly find we are this shining, beautiful gem called Soul.

Soul Becoming Godlike

Soul, a particle of God, is blessed with the gift of creative imagination, which finds a solution for every problem.

You are Soul. You are a special being, as is your neighbor.

Back in early Christian times, Jesus said, "Love thy neighbour as thyself." He wasn't saying that you should love yourself more than your neighbor. He said, "Love thy neighbour as thyself," because generally, Soul's evolution is such that a person first learns to love himself or herself.

Often, it's a very egotistical, selfish kind of love.

At times it comes in the form of showering oneself with wealth, finery, and pretty things. These things are not bad, but sometimes this becomes the goal and the substance of living. And it is not.

The reason we're here, the reason we are like some gem hidden inside this shell of sand, being ground down, is so that we can become godlike.

This grinding by life works on the pretensions that we have, on our vanity. And gradually we become more of a light—more of a spiritual light—to ourselves and to others.

Godlike Element in Soul

In ECK, through the spiritual exercises and your experiences in the dream state and with Soul Travel, the expansion of consciousness, you can go back to find some of the reasons, the past life, that brought these problems to you today. Or if they're caused by something in this lifetime, something that happened maybe a week or a month ago, you can zero in on that too. You can find out what happened, what you did. It might be a bad situation at work or a problem in a personal relationship. Sometimes it's not something you're doing now, but a reaction someone is having to something you've done to him or her in the past.

But at least you have something to work with. You have the creative power within you. This is the godlike element within each Soul.

The ECK, the Holy Spirit, is the creative power of Light and Sound. This is the Voice of God, and Soul was made from the Light and Sound. In other words, the creative power is in each human being. Therefore each human being has the inborn ability to take charge of his or her own life and not dwell in the victim consciousness that is so popular in some circles today.

Working beyond the Symptoms

When Divine Spirit does something to help us, it's not simply to cure a symptom. It goes to the cause, the cause that has been lying inside you for centuries from past lives.

Today so many Western doctors are trained to treat symptoms. This is mainstream medicine, and it's very necessary and helpful in its own way. But some of the alternate ways of healing try to work with the causes of an illness.

In the same way, the Mahanta, the Living ECK Master tries to work beyond the symptoms of why a person is having a hard time in this life. The Mahanta is an expression of the Spirit of God that is always with you. It is also a title of the Living ECK Master, who is both an inner and outer teacher who can lead Soul back home to God. The Mahanta goes back into the past and brings the problems to the front, and he gives them to the seeker of truth to work out as the seeker is able to.

Beam Me Up, Scotty!

"Josh" felt that his relationship with the Inner Master was such that anytime he had a bad experience, he could simply say, "Mahanta, please fix this." And the problem would be magically resolved.

One night Josh had a dream about the old *Star Trek* series. In the dream he is Captain Kirk of the starship *Enterprise*. Enemy Klingons are holding him captive on a strange planet while the starship circles above.

The Living ECK Master, in the role of

Scotty, is in charge of the transporter. The dreaded Klingons have taken away Captain Kirk's communicator. Luckily, he has a little electronic device hidden in his back pocket. He uses it now to signal the starship in Morse code. "Scotty, beam me up!" Over and over he sends his distress signal to the starship, but things are getting tense.

Off in the distance Josh sees a battered little truck, raising a dust cloud behind it as it chugs its way toward him. Behind the wheel is the Living ECK Master, playing the role of Scotty.

Scotty slams on the brakes and jumps out. He grabs Captain Kirk, pushes him into the back of the truck, and takes off, driving back down the road in the direction he'd just come from.

Josh calls out to the Mahanta, the Living ECK Master, "Scotty, beam us up!"

"Listen," the Living ECK Master says, "I drove for thirty-five hours to get here. We're not going back the easy way!"

The dream helped Josh realize he had a problem. He was being held captive by the passions of the mind. Until he could be free of them, he wouldn't get back to the starship, which symbolized the spiritual freedom to travel the worlds of God.

TAKE RESPONSIBILITY FOR YOUR LIFE

My job, my mission, is not to do things for other people in the line of healing or prophecies.

But many of you are more ready and able to begin moving seriously on the path to God than you have ever been before. This means that you learn to take responsibility for your own life, for your own health, for your own economics. You try to become self-sufficient.

It doesn't mean that you're never going to be short of money, that you're always going to have good health, or that you're always going to be feeling perfect and cheery every day. It doesn't mean that. It does mean that you recognize the responsibility for being where you are, that it's somehow to do with your state of consciousness. That if you want to change any outer condition, the changes must first come within yourself. That somehow you have to look at life differently from the way you have in the past.

The ways you've been looking at life in the past are what have brought you the problem today. The past can be as recent as yesterday or as long ago as your birth or a previous life.

What Causes Our Problems?

Each person has a whole series of experiences—good and bad—from the past. Our particular combination of experiences is what makes each one of us a unique individual, different from anyone else.

Many of these experiences were caused by our own thoughts and expectations. Right or wrong, the wheels of life were then set in motion to bring us the experiences we needed to manifest our state of consciousness.

Soul enters the human form and begins Its first earthly lives in a state of consciousness bordering on the naive and innocent.

The individual believes the best of his fellow man. But as he goes through a progression of lives, he often becomes increasingly narrow and suspicious, sometimes falling under the influence of the dark forces.

In one way or another, he goes through the whole range of experiences. He is pulled left and right, back and forth, over and over throughout many lifetimes.

Gradually, he begins to be aware of the pain of living through these experiences of his own making. And when this occurs, he slowly comes to an understanding: He alone is responsible for his actions.

Identifying Our Problems

On the path of ECK, we learn to identify the problems that are plaguing us. The Inner Master begins to open up small scenes from our past. We sometimes perceive these as disjointed dreams. These dream experiences give us a way to start finding out who and what we are.

As we move into the higher states of consciousness, we become more aware of our responsibility—first of all to ourselves, but also to other people. Our responsibility to others is mainly to allow them the same freedom we want for ourselves.

Pay Now, and Be Done with It

"Nick" had a dream in which a beautiful young woman came to the office. She was trying to use the phone on his manager's desk. Nick and the girl felt an immediate attraction for each other in the dream, and soon they began a passionate romance. But, to his frustration, it led nowhere.

Then he awoke.

Some weeks later, a young student came to the office to get work experience. Nick loved her from the start. He did everything in his power to win her heart, but she coyly brushed aside his passion with promises. Later, always later. Soon everyone in the office was talking about their relationship.

Then the sky fell in.

Through the office grapevine, Nick learned that this young woman had been having a secret love affair with his best friend at work. It had begun nearly the first week that she had arrived there. Worse, Nick had set the stage. One night that first week, he had to work late, so he asked his good friend to take her home. That was the beginning of the end.

Only the ECK, Divine Spirit, kept Nick from losing his mind when he learned of the secret love affair. But he turned sour on life. Why had this beautiful young woman come—to purposely bring him grief?

In his anxiety and anger, he even forgot about the spiritual love of the Mahanta, the Living ECK Master.

Then came a second dream. The Mahanta took him on the Time Track and showed him a past life in which he had been a woman. Married to a wealthy man, this individual had two house servants, both of whom suffered due to Nick's misuse of position and authority. One was this student.

"You made that karma," the Mahanta explained. "That debt stands between you and God's love. Pay now, and be done with it."

In the end, Nick recognized the hand of karma and the long, outstanding debt that he needed to settle. It took awhile for the crushing pain to subside, of course, but now he's happy he settled the debt. After the pain had finally gone, Nick felt a new sense of freedom and lightness.

God's love could now shine more directly into his heart. That obstructing block of karmic debt was gone.

How to Handle Problems

In a crisis of any kind, it is generally not understood why certain people benefit.

For instance, when the stock market crashes, there are people who become rich. Why? Because every time a big bubble is created in the regular pattern of human activity, those who understand the laws—whether of economics or politics or anything else—can use the energy to advance their own careers.

In a spiritual sense, if you have problems and catastrophes in your own life, this energy can propel you to spiritual heights. Letters come to me from people begging to be spared problems in life. They are looking toward the old concept of God: If something goes wrong in their life, they say, "Lord, please deliver me from it." They are deaf to the question, "But what will you do in return?" They think it is enough to say, "In return I'll love you and worship you." It's not enough.

We have to take full responsibility for our own lives. Once we do, we find that the problems we have are ones we can handle. Not only that, but we can often choose our problems.

You may think if there were a choice between problems and no problems, you'd choose to have no problems, and I'd say you would be very wise. Unfortunately, this world doesn't run like that. It works by degrees, not absolutes. You can't say you will or will not have problems. That's absolute, and life doesn't work that way. It works like this: You are going to have problems, but you now have a choice as to how to handle them.

You can choose a short-term solution that will make you feel good for a day or two. But it's not going to work out so well in the long run.

You have a choice: You can handle the problem with a good solution or a poor solution. If you don't have self-discipline, you say, "Here today, gone tomorrow; I may not be around in a week." So you take the short-term solution. A week later you're still alive, and you have to pay the piper. And then it's, "O Lord, why me? Why have you done this to me? Someone else must be responsible, certainly not I."

Just like Job in the Old Testament, you can cry and curse the day you were born. You might even blame the devil for your misfortune.

Responsibility is the key.

Figuring Out a Problem

One summer a group of ECKists were having a retreat at a YWCA camp up in Canada.

They had a good time with the activities and meetings. But Saturday evening the camp director, who was not an ECKist, made an announcement.

"We've lost our fresh water supply," she said. There would be no showers that night.

A groan went up from everyone. They had been outdoors all day, and although camp is camp, it still feels good to have a shower. But there was no water. And the camp director didn't know what to do.

One of the ECKists, "Ted," was a mechanical engineer. He went to the camp director and offered his help, and she was glad to accept it. She led him to the pump house and opened the door. Ted just looked at the maze of pipes inside and wondered where to begin. So he said inwardly to the Mahanta, "Let me see if I can work through this logically."

The Mahanta is the inner guide of the initiates in ECK. It's the inner side of myself, the person who appears in dreams and teaches you there, who gives you the secret teachings of ECK. On the outer I give you what I can, but it's mostly to make a connection for those of you who are ready, willing, and able to go into the other worlds in your dreams, for those who want to know about truth, know about divine love, know about wisdom and many other things that are available for Soul to gain on Its path home to God.

This knowledge is available. But many times people in ECK call upon the Mahanta for help or protection.

In this case, Ted needed help figuring out a problem. The camp wasn't getting any water, which was an inconvenience for a great number of people. Nothing serious, but—if you will pardon the expression—it was enough to dampen the weekend.

Reversing the Flow

Ted checked the pipes, did some tests, and found that the two water softeners in the pump house had plugged up. The backwash cycle wasn't working. A water softener has to go through a cycle to cleanse itself; it has to reverse the flow of water.

Because this cleansing cycle wasn't happening in the two water softeners, the water flow to the showers had stopped. So the ECKist was able to fix the problem by bypassing the two water softeners. When he told the others they could take showers now, everyone cheered.

Then one of them asked, "What was the problem?"

Ted explained that the flow had to be reversed. And since this was a meeting of ECK initiates, they all knew what he was talking about.

When people first come to the path of ECK or any other religion, they are so used to asking. They are used to begging God to fulfill their needs. Very few people ever think of giving something back to God, to life, or to others. The ECKists understood that when the engineer said the direction of the flow needed to be reversed, it was now time to give.

It was now time to give of themselves, their talents, and the divine love of the Holy Spirit that was flowing through them. It was time to give to others.

Law of Reversed Effort

If you feel you are trying too hard to accomplish something, consider the Law of Reversed Effort. This law is a practical law of nature concerned with the use of the imaginative powers.

It goes like this: The more you concentrate on putting your imaginative powers upon something, the less you are able to do it. Or, the harder one struggles to avoid something, the more it will be attracted to him.

For example, when one is trying to ride a bicycle and avoid hitting any rocks on the road, he is so conscious of hitting the rocks he'll probably do so. Or if a person tries to walk across a small plank from one building to another at the tenth floor, his mind would be on falling, not on walking.

This law is concerned with imagining and feeling. The negative thoughts are apt to be more effective than the positive, because the negative usually has more feeling with it.

Take your goal into contemplation, and focus on relaxing, letting go the negative feelings associated with not achieving this goal. Set up a positive image about the goal, then put feeling with it. It's that simple.

This is a form of spiritual exercise.

Spiritual Exercises: Key to Problem Solving

Spiritual exercises link you with the guidance of the Holy Spirit, which is seen as Light and heard as Sound. The inner Sound is the Voice of God calling us home. The inner Light is a beacon to light our way. All the Spiritual Exercises of ECK are built on these two divine aspects of the Holy Spirit.

They work similarly to physical exercises. If you want your body to be strong and healthy, you've got to swim or run or do something to keep fit. For the Soul body, you do the Spiritual Exercises of ECK, a form of inner communication also called contemplation.

Learning spiritual consciousness is learning how to live in this world no matter what comes. We learn through these spiritual exercises how to live life graciously, from childhood to old age. We learn how to live life in the best way possible.

The Spiritual Exercises of ECK give you confidence in yourself. You learn that you are Soul, you are eternal. Then you know with certainty that you live forever, that death cannot destroy you.

When you do the Spiritual Exercises of ECK, fill yourself with love and goodwill.

Be patient with yourself. It is a rare person who has instant success and dramatic results right away. Expect subtle, gradual changes in your outlook on life over a period of weeks or months. A good way to keep track of this is by using a journal to note any insights, perceptions, or changes you notice in yourself.

Connect with the Divine by Singing *HU*

One of the most powerful spiritual exercises I can give you is to sing *HU.*

HU is an ancient name for God. It can be sung as a love song to God. All that we do with the word *HU* is sing it with reverence. It represents the enormous love that the Creator has for Its creation.

HU can be sung by anyone, whether Christian, Muslim, or of any other religion. It isn't meant to change your religion. HU will enhance it.

It is the sound of all sounds. It is the wind in the leaves, falling rain, thunder of jets, singing of birds, the awful rumble of a tornado. Again, Its sound is heard in laughter, weeping, the din of city traffic, ocean waves, and the quiet rippling of a mountain stream.

Singing *HU* can bring comfort, peace, and calm. It can also bring expanded awareness, a release from fears, and answers to your questions.

It Will Always Work If You Keep Your Heart Open

This story is about "Ginger." She's from Florida, and she recently retired. Since then, she's been working as an ecotour guide.

One of these tours is designed so that the tourists will leave as small an imprint on the environment as possible. In other words, they may go in and look at the land or parks, but they'll try to leave no trace of themselves. They don't want to damage the ecology. They even try to improve it.

Anyway, Ginger joined a group of ten other guides. It was the start of a new school session, and a class of handicapped children wanted to go on one of the tours. Now, these kids were physically, emotionally, and mentally handicapped in one way or another. The tour boss said to these tour guides, "Would anyone like to volunteer for this tour?"

No hands went up, because none of them felt really sure that they were capable of doing a thorough job. How do you work with so many kids who are not just physically handicapped, but also emotionally and mentally handicapped, all together in one group? How do you work with such a broad range of consciousness? The tour guides weren't thinking in those words, of course. They were just wondering, Are we up to it? They didn't think so.

So the tour boss said, "Well, Ginger, I'm going to assign them to you. Would you do it?"

Ginger said, "I'd be happy to." Except that wasn't quite so. Ginger had the same doubts that the others had. Besides that, she was the newest one there. She had just led a couple of tours so far, and they'd gone OK, but this was a big step. So she wasn't real sure.

This tour was to take place Monday morning, and Ginger had a lot of time to get ready for it. She got prepared and went to the rendezvous area very early on Monday morning. She had set everything up. Now she was ready.

The phone rang. It was the teacher at the school. She said, "The school board has canceled this tour because they feel it would be too dangerous for these children to be near the water." The location was somewhere near the Gulf of Mexico. And Ginger said, "But we're not going to be anywhere near the water."

The teacher said, "It's too late to reschedule this tour because there are just too many board members to get hold of, and then we'll need time to see if we can reach a consensus. It's too late for today. But I'll get back to you if something turns up."

Later that very same day, the teacher called the tour boss and said, "Once the school board heard the tour wasn't near water, they said everything was OK, and you can go ahead with the tour. So, when's a good time for you? We can be there on Thursday morning." The tour boss asked Ginger, "Are you up to it?"

Ginger said, "Sure, I'll do it."

Ginger's Inner Preparation

Ginger had done her spiritual exercises in the meantime. She wondered, *What did I miss? Why was this tour canceled on Monday?* And then she realized she had prepared everything except herself—spiritually. She hadn't asked the Inner Master, the Mahanta, what she should do to prepare.

During her spiritual exercise, the Master now said to her, "Open your heart. Invite these kids to the event on the inner planes." And Ginger did. Then, all the way to the rendezvous point on Thursday morning, she also sang *HU*. She sang *HU* the whole way.

A little bit later, the bus came and dropped the kids off. Ginger and the kids got along fine. They were completely comfortable with each other. The tour turned out to be a smashing success.

The teacher was so happy that she wrote an e-mail to Ginger's boss and said how grateful she was for the care and consideration that Ginger had shown for the children. And the children had loved it. They would like to do it again.

Such commendations didn't come in often, so the boss forwarded the e-mail to all the other tour guides. One of the other tour guides came up to Ginger and asked, "What did you do to make that work?"

Ginger didn't have much time to tell her right at that moment, but she said, "I did a spiritual exercise. This is how I did it. Then I sang *HU*." She mentioned things like open your heart, inwardly invite the kids during the spiritual exercise, and sing *HU* all the way to the rendezvous point.

Then Ginger gave the tour guide a *HU: A Love Song to God* CD. She said, "Here's a CD. You can listen to it yourself so you know how it goes." Now another teacher had been touched by this.

So Ginger's lessons included such things as: open your heart, listen to the Inner Master, and above all, be grateful for the blessings the Master gives you.

Later Ginger had another tour. This was with a group of children who had no handicaps at all. Ginger did the same thing as she had before, with the same results. And this group's teacher, too, wrote a note to the tour boss and said, "The kids had a wonderful time. We'd like to do this again. We'd like to commend Ginger because she was so open."

This technique worked for Ginger whether it was used for one category of children or another category. I'm sure she found that it would work even when there were adults in the tours. It will always work—if she keeps her heart open, invites people to come to the event during her spiritual exercise, and sings *HU* all the way there.

How To Sing *HU*

With eyes open or closed, take a few deep breaths to relax. Then begin to sing *HU* (pronounced like the word *hue*) in a long, drawn-out sound: HU-U-U-U.

Take another breath, and sing *HU* again. Continue for up to twenty minutes. Sing *HU* with a feeling of love, and it will gradually open your heart to God.

Do this exercise every day. Spend about twenty minutes on it. This builds your spiritual stamina gently over time. Regular daily practice is the key to success.

Also, when your day is hard, remember to sing *HU*. It puts you back in line with the Holy Spirit.

When you sing *HU*, you are saying to

Divine Spirit, "I've opened myself to you. Give me the understanding and the wisdom to meet the waves of life, and the problems, troubles, and whatever else. Give me the strength to meet life." This is basically all that we do when we do a Spiritual Exercise of ECK.

This Is Why We Have Problems

When things are not being resolved in the way a person thinks they should, he might feel that Divine Spirit, the ECK, doesn't work. The ECK may be working out the best possible solution that will bring about a greater overall change. But he doesn't see it, simply because he is looking at the problem from the lower state of consciousness. He has judged the situation from his limited viewpoint.

People with this attitude will always have trouble in their lives. They may ask for help and receive it. But just as quickly as the problem is resolved, they forget they ever had it and immediately slip out of the Light and Sound.

The Light and Sound are not just words. The Light is actually seen in the dream state, during Soul Travel, or in a spiritual exercise. It comes in a great range of colors, from blue to pink to brilliant white. Usually we see the higher colors in ECK.

This is the Light of God coming in and purifying Soul. The other aspect, the Sound, is actually heard by the individual. It may sound like a flute, buzzing bees, twittering sparrows, a choir singing, or the wind blowing—any of these things.

The Light and Sound are the only way the Holy Spirit, which we call the ECK, can be seen or heard by man. The closest It comes to a human voice is when these twin aspects come together in a matrix into the form of the Inner Master, the Mahanta. We don't hear etheric voices from the clouds, proclaim the Lord spoke to us, or claim to receive instructions that dictate what others should do. When we do get a feeling about something that has to be done, we examine our feeling carefully to determine that the act is not going to impede anyone on the path to God. If it does, then it's wrong. If it somehow uplifts another person and doesn't affect their freedom, then it's a good act.

Of course, the imperfect human consciousness wants to believe it's always right, and this is why we have problems.

A Crisis Is an Opportunity in Disguise

A solution is hidden in the folds of every reverse. No matter what is thrown into our face, there is a way to roll with the punch.

People with a high state of consciousness are not frozen into inaction by terror brought about through disasters. They immediately make a plan to turn the negative energy to advantage. At this level of creative imagination, Soul is in a condition of survival.

The lesson of the worlds of matter is to develop Soul's ability to ride the crests of life.

Peanut's Hard Road to Freedom

Peanut, a rabbit, belongs to an ECK member we'll call Willow. She had been given the rabbit by somebody who asked, "Do you want a one-and-a-half-year-old rabbit?"

She said, "Sure."

Willow hadn't had a rabbit since she was a child, and she thought it would be really nice to have one for a pet.

In American Indian lore, a rabbit is the epitome of fear. There's nothing quite as afraid of life as a rabbit, because it really has nothing to defend itself with. It has no sharp teeth. It can put up a fight, but it doesn't have natural defenses except speed. So the rabbit has to take advantage of speed.

Well, Willow brought the rabbit home. He came in a steel cage that clipped over a two-foot-square bottom pan. He sat in his cage all the first day.

The second day, when Willow took the cage top off to clean the pan, the rabbit just sat in the pan. He wouldn't leave, although he could have free run of the kitchen. Suddenly she got a certain feeling from the rabbit: the name Peanut came. She said, "I guess your name is Peanut."

After that she called him Peanut. He was a little brown rabbit, and he didn't really want to jump around the kitchen. So she took him up to the bedroom and set him down there. And Peanut moved very carefully around the room, testing this new freedom. Until now, he had known only his little cage. There's not too much freedom in a cage.

All of a sudden Peanut ran around the room. And in the middle of the room, he jumped straight up in the air. It was his joy at this sense of freedom.

Willow was so happy for Peanut. She said, "Little Peanut has freedom and now knows joy."

She spent a few days sitting in her bedroom, reading a book and watching the rabbit. The rabbit would come over to her sometimes. Then she found out that rabbits like to eat paper and wood. And she also found she wasn't getting some of her other work done. She thought it would work out a little better if she took Peanut down to the kitchen.

So Willow put Peanut in the cage, took it down to the kitchen, and opened it. She expected the explosion of brown rabbit. She thought Peanut would pop right out of that cage and go running around the kitchen. But Peanut sat in the cage. He wouldn't move, wouldn't budge.

She tried everything. She brought a little rug over and set him on the rug. But as soon as she let go of him, Peanut hopped right back in the cage. She'd take him out and set him on the rug again, and Peanut would hop back into the cage. She was trying to let him know, "You can run around the kitchen." She had the kitchen door blocked off so that he couldn't get into the other areas of the home.

All Peanut would do was stick his nose over the edge of the pan and just sniff. One day, he did a little hop to the rug, then went right back into the cage. Back and forth just a little bit.

Trying Out New Freedom

This isn't going real well, Willow thought. She had a spare room she was going to clean and paint. *Maybe we can spend more time together in there,* she thought.

It was kind of neutral ground between the

kitchen and the bedroom. The room was right across from her bedroom, and the rabbit seemed to get along OK there. After a while, she opened the door to let Peanut have the run of the house, but he would stop, just as if he had run into an electric fence. He would come right up to the doorway and stop. But Peanut wouldn't go through the door. Rabbit, again, signifies fear.

Willow didn't know what to do. She said, "I've tried to pull the rabbit out of his cage. He won't come. I've tried to pull him out of his room. He won't come. So I'll try to coax him."

She lay down in the doorway of the bedroom across from this third room and said, "Come on, Peanut. Come on, Peanut. You can do it!" All the rabbit had to do was hop out of the room and into the hallway.

Peanut wanted to come, but he didn't have the courage. One day, he finally got all his courage together. Peanut ran from that third room into the bedroom, ran around it a few times, ran back out in the hallway, and ran around there a couple times. Pretty soon, Peanut had the freedom to run in this third room and the bedroom and the hallway, just back and forth. And Peanut felt really good.

By the time Willow had written a letter to tell me this story, she said Peanut had the run of the house. In other words, Peanut had overcome his fear and could run throughout the house.

We Have Fear Too

Willow realized she was very much like Peanut. When she had first come into Eckankar, the Mahanta had taken her out of the cage, which was her own little world. He had taken the top off and said to her, "Here, you're free. You can run around in this bigger room." But she was afraid and didn't want to step out of her own comfortable little world.

Gradually, the Mahanta tried to show her there was nothing to fear, that there was a greater room and a greater world outside.

Trying to pull Peanut out of the cage didn't work, any more than it did for the Master to take Willow out in the dream state. So finally the Master just coaxed and encouraged her. And she was able to accept the greater spiritual freedom that she found in Eckankar.

A Spiritual Exercise for Viewing Difficulties

This exercise allows you to see why long-lasting or hard-to-solve problems are still with you.

In contemplation, look at your problem and ask yourself which of these viewpoints you hold about it.

1. You view the problem as a battering ram. When it approaches, you fall over backward, flattened to the ground.
2. You view the problem as a vital, valuable lesson which will teach you something. You believe it will become a spiritual springboard to

give you the necessary incentive and energy to climb up and out of your present situation.

Your attitude about your problem holds the key to whether your experience with it will be easy or difficult, long or short.

Those people who have spiritual success don't say, "Oh, no!" and fall down when a problem comes up. They look to see the reason or lesson behind it. They ask the Mahanta, "What can I learn from it? How has it made me stronger?"

The ECK sometimes works very subtly. Often we do not recognize what It is trying to tell us. We're too busy being afraid or angry to see the humor in the situations that life uses to teach us what we must learn about ourselves.

ECK may not always provide a fast way to learn, but it does provide a sure way to learn.

Compromise: A Good Solution

Abraham Lincoln was actually a very funny man, but as the duties of the presidency began to weigh on him, the humor didn't always show. He also had a very sharp intellect, which is how the ECK comes through as one works on the Mental Plane. He consistently came up with clever ways to work out difficult situations, occasionally even finding himself in the role of Solomon.

While he was still practicing law, a farmer came to Lincoln's office, obviously very upset. "Sir," the man said, "I want to file for divorce."

"Why?" Lincoln asked.

"My wife and I used to get along very well," the farmer began. "We lived in a log cabin at first, but as times got better, we were able to build ourselves a nice frame house."

Lincoln was puzzled. "A lot of people would be happy to move from a log cabin to a frame house," he said. "So what's the problem?"

The farmer said, "I want to paint the house white like the rest of our neighbors, but my wife wants to paint it brown."

"That sounds easy enough to resolve," Lincoln said. "Why don't you just figure out some compromise?"

"It's way beyond that," the farmer said. "What began as a mild dispute has turned into a violent argument. She's broken dishes over my head and even poured hot water down my back!"

Abe Lincoln thought it over for a moment. Finally he said, "Surely you must have learned something from life. There has to be some solution to this problem. Before you do anything drastic, why not go home and try to work out a compromise?"

The farmer was reluctant. As far as he was concerned, it was a lost cause. "At least give it a try," Lincoln urged. "Then come back in a month, and we'll talk again."

Four weeks later the farmer returned to Lincoln's office. "It all worked out," he announced.

"You and your wife reached a compromise?" Lincoln asked. He was always eager to hear how his advice turned out.

"We sure did," the man said, looking mighty pleased with himself.

"How did you do it?"

The farmer said. "We agreed to paint the house brown."

We go through life wanting things our own way. But all too often we run into others who disagree with us. Words lead to more words, until finally we are in such a predicament that we can't back off—to do so would mean we'd lose face. Yet, one of the biggest lessons we can learn in ECK is to do everything possible to reach an accord with the individual with whom we are having a problem. But that doesn't mean it's always going to work.

After lengthy negotiations between the United States and Russia fell through, the media approached John Foster Dulles, secretary of state during the Eisenhower administration, and demanded an explanation.

"Why did you let the negotiations fail?" they asked.

"Gentlemen," he said, "it takes two sides to reach an agreement."

In ECK, as we come out of the childhood of spirituality and move into the greater states of awareness, we learn to let other people be. So even when it simply is not possible to reach an agreement, we can still figure out ways to make the situation livable for ourself and others.

How to Dry Up the Karmic Stream

It sounds paradoxical, but when we have a problem, we don't call on God to solve it for us. We dig into our own resources, knowing that the solution to every problem is hidden within the problem itself. This is all there is to it.

Most of you may not believe it, but if you're poor, somehow you have the ability to pull yourself out of the hole. For too long we have been led to believe that some omnipotent power might miraculously appear and hand us a million dollars. People like to dream about winning a big sweepstakes, and occasionally some do.

But why waste your life dreaming about someday when you can be building your own world now? This is something you are going to have to learn before you can leave the lower worlds of karma and reincarnation.

The only way we can buy our way out of here is by the accumulation of good karma. In ECK this means doing all things in the name of the Mahanta—or in the name of God. You can simply say, "I am not doing this action for my own benefit or for the benefit of anyone else; I am doing this in the name of God." Then you go and do it, and you don't worry about it.

This is the way we start to dry up the karmic stream that runs through us. As it dries up, the conditions of our life have to change. It won't always be for the better at first, because as we begin working off karma, we also gain the capacity to work off more. But once much of the karma has begun to work off, we find we are better able to live this life and move forward with happiness and confidence as we make our way to God.

This is the way to freedom.

A Spiritual Exercise to Start the Day Right

You may find it helpful to declare yourself a vehicle for God each morning. Just make a statement such as, "I declare myself a vehicle for God." Or you can use the ECK terms: "I declare myself a vehicle for the SUGMAD" (which is God), "the ECK" (or Spirit), "and the Mahanta" (which is this high state of consciousness that we look to).

Then go about your duties throughout the rest of the day.

You don't even have to think about it anymore. You know that every experience you have today is for your spiritual unfoldment. If a negative situation comes up with your fellow employees or what have you, there is a way to handle it.

You will find that declaring yourself a vehicle for Spirit and God is a great help in giving you an understanding of the purpose of your everyday life.

You'll also find it will help take those tangles out of the stomach in the morning, when you have to go to work but would rather not.

Creative-Process Spiritual Exercise

To solve problems, work with the creative cycle in ECK. When you come up against something, try to put it into a question.

On the other planes, sometimes the Mahanta, the Living ECK Master sits at a table with the rest of the ECK Masters, and they talk things out. According to the way we regard ECK Masters, any one of them ought to be smart enough to handle anything that goes on. So why do they talk things out?

This is simply an educational process. We learn what a Master does and how he works with the ECK, or Divine Spirit. How do you work with the ECK? It's easy to say, "Just let the ECK take care of it," then sit back and wait. But that is not always going to work. A better way is as follows.

First, figure out what's wrong and say, "Something's going wrong. This is the title I've given to what's going wrong. Now I would like an answer for how it can go right."

Next, contemplate on the problem and look at it from every angle. You may talk it over with everybody who's got the least bit of knowledge about it. Eventually, if you ask a good question, the answer is going to suggest itself.

At some point, it's going to become very clear what to do.

Questions and Answers

As spiritual leader of Eckankar, I get thousands of letters from seekers of truth around the world. All want direct and useful answers about how to travel the road to God. Here are several questions I've been asked about how to deal with problems.

Read on for clues that might help you.

Why Do We Have Problems?

Can you explain why we have problems?

Troubles that come to us are for our purification. They come to us because we must learn a divine law.

Divine Spirit will use the most negative situations to teach us, and we wonder, *Why has God forsaken me?* God has not forsaken us. We are unwilling to give up certain passions of the mind and take the next step in our spiritual development. Habits fall away once Soul decides It really wants spiritual realization more than Its vices.

The spiritual life is not meant to finally end the succession of problems, for they are given as opportunities for Soul's unfoldment. What the spiritual student does develop, however, is the inner link with the ECK, the Holy Spirit. Thus he taps into the Supreme Creative Force that guides him around all the blocks in his path that once defeated him.

One's ability to take charge of his own life increases. This is a solid step toward self-mastery and that state of consciousness called the kingdom of heaven.

How Do You Help People Solve Problems?

If someone is feeling scared or hurt inside, how do you help them, and how can you listen to so many?

Let's look at your first question. There are two ways to help people solve a problem: do it for them, or let them do most or all of it alone.

Which way do you think gives them more experience to care for themselves, to survive? And which way do you think builds the most confidence?

The second way, of course.

So the Mahanta, the Living ECK Master prefers to use the second method, unless there is a great, immediate need to help someone who is unable to do it alone. Either way, however, is an ECK miracle.

Second question . . .

The Master helps people overcome fear by showing them a way to solve or lessen their fearful situation. He gives hope. He grants ideas. He may send others to offer aid. He may also remove a threat with an out-and-out miracle.

And how to help those who hurt inside? He brings love. It comes to fill a heart in its darkest hour. Or, again, he may appear in a dream to show the karmic reason for the pain.

To see the root of a problem is often all it takes to make a hurt fly away.

And, last, how does the Master listen to so many? It's all about the Rod of ECK Power. It makes the Master one with the Holy Spirit, so he has all Its qualities, like the ability to be anywhere and everywhere there is a spiritual need.

Attitudes Create Your World

Why don't troubles go away once we ask for help?

Much of the trouble we have in life is a result of some long-standing negative attitude. It has created these situations. Soul gains experience as It works through these rough spots on the road.

Some of our troubles will be dispelled

by Divine Spirit while others are not. They are part of the divine plan for Soul to gain the purification or change in consciousness so It can know what It is. It needs to know why It has reincarnated into today's family and business environment.

Many people do not understand that life, with its burdens, is a treasure. The weight of disappointment makes us close our eyes to the gift of being in the world to learn about the loving heart.

Problems with a Friend

A friend is always trying to draw me into her conflicts. How do I handle this problem, since she is very close to me?

There are people who try to draw others into their problems. Their own troubles are overwhelming because they like the attention from others.

Of course, how much you choose to become a part of her world is for you to decide. But don't feel guilty if you want to pull out of the situation because it interferes with your life.

She has to make up her own mind about personal decisions. If her inner guidance gives her a direction, fine. All her decisions have to be her own.

You may act as a listening post if you want to. But don't let her take your life away from you.

Relationship Problems

I have been having recurring dreams which involve me, my boyfriend, and another woman. In all the dreams, my boyfriend treats me like extra baggage and ignores me while paying attention to her.

We have been having difficulties in our relationship, and for some reason, I don't trust him. How can I tell whether my dreams are intuitive or simply represent my insecurities?

A relationship without trust won't last.

What is the source of this mistrust? Does he look at other women when you are out together in public?

Dreams can prepare you for a relationship that may be coming to an end. They will tell you something is wrong. If your partner is showing less affection toward you, you must decide whether to try to patch up the relationship or let it go.

Think of your dreams as advisers. They may point out problems and offer solutions, but consider all the facts before deciding on any important issue.

Especially watch people's daily behavior toward you. Your dreams may suggest what behavior to look out for, but don't break up a relationship without some physical evidence to back up your suspicions.

No matter what happens with this relationship, try to be a greater channel for divine love. Love will overcome suspicion, which can destroy any relationship.

Rising from Failure

I am depressed over the condition I find my life in. I cannot even look for a job because I am afraid I would just be bored with it, and I am not able to face another failure. What can I do?

Sit down and list the things you like and do not like about yourself, in separate columns. Look at them once a month. As you review the past thirty days, look for any changes the Holy Spirit has brought to you.

Self-discipline is an absolute necessity if one is to have a productive life. Replace old tastes and preferences with new, better ones. But do it in the name of God, with love and a sincere heart, or nothing will come of this experiment.

You must also look at how you wish to spend your time at work. Plot out a rough plan for getting (and holding) a job that has the things in it needed to keep your interest. Take care of the outer needs of the body because they are important for a sense of well-being. What you want to do is live the complete life.

The Spiritual Exercises of ECK build up spiritual momentum for Soul to realize the godlike being It is; therefore, it is imperative you do them for a twenty-minute period every day. If you have the discipline for that, I will certainly be with you at all times.

Writing to the Master: A Spiritual Exercise

I'd like to leave you with one final exercise.

So often, people say, "I simply cannot deal with my life. Everything is wrong. I can't get over this problem."

Sit down and write a personal letter to the Master. You don't have to be a member of Eckankar. You don't have to mail it. Now this is important: When you're feeling very upset and down on the world, when you don't have the confidence you want or you're feeling at odds with people, this is the time to sit down somewhere and write. You don't have to mail it, as I said.

I'm emphasizing this because you'll find that the Mahanta works inwardly with each person. You don't have to understand how it works because that isn't important.

All you have to understand is whether it works for you. If it works for you, that's all that matters because your spiritual unfoldment is at stake here. Your spiritual freedom and your greater sense of receiving divine love.

First, write down very clearly what's bothering you. Do this in the first or second paragraph. Even the first or second sentence if you can. Say, "This is what's troubling me. I can't handle it." Then keep writing some of the experiences that have happened that support the problem you're having. Say, "I'm having this certain problem with somebody at work. And here are some of the things that this person has done to me."

Write it down. And as you write, after

about five, ten, or fifteen minutes, you're going to find that something's lifting from you. You will definitely feel something lifting.

If it's a really bad problem, you may have to write for fifteen or twenty minutes, not just five or ten. You'll feel something lifting. The problem won't be as heavy as it was before. And if this feeling of depression comes back again—in a day or two, a week, or a month—sit down and write about it again. This requires self-discipline.

This is one of the steps to self-mastery: learning how to have the discipline to very directly face what's causing you trouble.

Put it down on a piece of paper in the first two sentences. Put in the details. You can do this with a voice recorder too, or on the computer. It doesn't make any difference. Just get it out.

The creative flow goes on all the time. You learn that no matter where you are or what the problem is, the first step to the solution is always within reach. If you don't have the answer yourself, ask around. Somebody near you will come up with ideas to get you started, and you can take it from there.

You do the best you can on your own, and by tapping into the ECK, It will tell you what to do next. The ECK works in even the simplest areas of your life.

You have the potential and the capability to become much more than you are now.

Once you open yourself to the Holy Spirit within, you can become an eagle in ECK, the experienced being, fully trained and qualified to become a Co-worker with God.

Next Steps in Spiritual Exploration

- **Try a spiritual exercise.**
  Review the spiritual exercises in this book or on our Web site.
  Experiment with them.
- **Browse our Web site: www.Eckankar.org.**
  Watch videos; get free books, answers to FAQs, and more info.
- **Attend an Eckankar event in your area.**
  Visit "Eckankar around the World" on our Web site.
- **Read additional books** about the ECK teachings.
- **Explore advanced spiritual study** with the Eckankar discourses that come with membership.
- **Call or write to us:** Call 1-800-LOVE GOD (1-800-568-3463, toll-free, automated) or (952) 380-2200 (direct).
- Write to: ECKANKAR, Dept. BK129, PO Box 2000, Chanhassen, MN 55317-2000 USA.

For Further Reading
By Harold Klemp

ECK Wisdom on Conquering Fear

Would having more courage and confidence help you make the most of this lifetime?

Going far beyond typical self-help advice, this booklet invites you to explore divine love as the antidote to anxiety and the doorway to inner freedom.

You will discover ways to identify the karmic roots of fear and align with your highest ideals.

Use this book to soar beyond your limitations and reap the benefits of self-mastery.

Live life to its fullest potential!

Spiritual Wisdom on Health and Healing

This booklet is rich with spiritual keys to better health on every level.

Discover the spiritual roots of illness and how gratitude can open your heart to God's love and healing.

Simple spiritual exercises go deep to help you get personal divine guidance and insights.

Revitalize your connection with the true healing power of God's love.

Spiritual Wisdom on Relationships

Find the answers to common questions of the heart, including the truth about Soul mates, how to strengthen a marriage, and how to know if a partnership is worth developing.

The spiritual exercises included in this booklet can help you break a pattern of poor relationships and find balance. You'll learn new ways to open your heart to love and enrich your relationship with God.

This booklet is a key for anyone wanting more love to give, more love to get, and better relationships with everyone in your life.

Spiritual Wisdom on Prayer, Meditation, and Contemplation

Bring balance and wonder to your life!

This booklet is a portal to your direct, personal connection with Divine Spirit.

Harold Klemp shows how you can experience the powerful benefits of contemplation—"a conversation with the most secret, most genuine, and most mysterious part of yourself."

Move beyond traditional meditation via dynamic spiritual exercises. Learn about the uplifting chant of HU (an ancient holy name for God), visualization, creative imagination, and other active techniques.

Spiritual Wisdom on Karma and Reincarnation

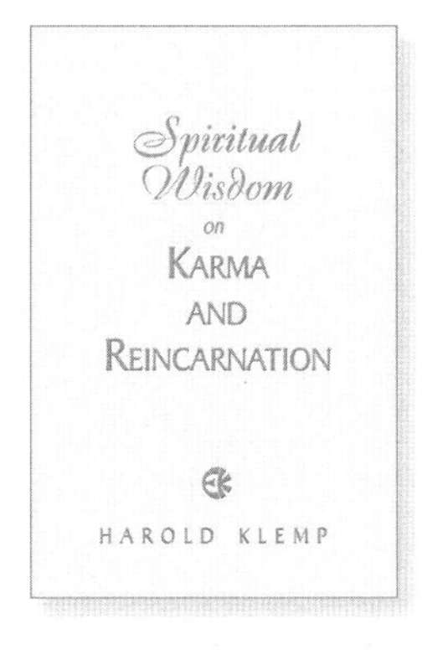

Have you lived before? What is the real meaning of life?

Discover your divine destiny—to move beyond the limits of karma and reincarnation and gain spiritual freedom.

This booklet reveals the purpose of living and the keys to spiritual growth.

You'll find answers to age-old questions about fate, destiny, and free will. These gems of wisdom can enhance your relationships, health, and happiness—and offer the chance to resolve all your karma in this lifetime!

Spiritual Wisdom on Dreams

This dream study will help you be more *awake* than you've ever been!

Spiritual Wisdom on Dreams reveals the most ancient of dream teachings for a richer and more productive life today.

In this dynamic booklet, author Harold Klemp shows you how to remember your dreams, apply dream wisdom to everyday situations, recognize prophetic dreams, and more.

You will be introduced to the art of dream interpretation and offered techniques to discover the treasures of your inner worlds.

ECK Wisdom on Life after Death

All that lies ahead is already within your heart.

ECK Wisdom on Life after Death invites you to explore the eternal nature of you!

Author Harold Klemp offers you new perspectives on seeing heaven before you die, meeting with departed loved ones, near-death experiences, getting help from spiritual guides, animals in heaven, and dealing with grief.

Try the techniques and spiritual exercise included in this book to find answers and explore the secrets of life after death—for yourself.

ECK Wisdom on Inner Guidance

Looking for answers, guidance, protection?

Help can come as a nudge, a dream, a vision, or a quiet voice within you. This book offers new ways to connect with the ever-present guidance of ECK, the Holy Spirit. Start today!

Discover how to listen to the Voice of God; attune to your true self; work with an inner guide; benefit from dreams, waking dreams, and Golden-tongued Wisdom; and ignite your creativity to solve problems.

Each story, technique, and spiritual exercise is a doorway to greater confidence and love for life.

Open your heart and let God's voice speak to you!

The Call of Soul

Discover how to find spiritual freedom in this lifetime and the infinite world of God's love for you. Includes a CD with dream and Soul Travel techniques.

HU, the Most Beautiful Prayer

Singing *HU,* the ancient name for God, can open your heart and lead you to a new understanding of yourself. Includes a CD of the HU song.

Past Lives, Dreams, and Soul Travel

These stories and exercises help you find your true purpose, discover greater love than you've ever known, and learn that spiritual freedom is within reach.

The Spiritual Exercises of ECK

This book is a staircase with 131 steps leading to the doorway to spiritual freedom, self-mastery, wisdom, and love. A comprehensive volume of spiritual exercises for every need.

The Road to Spiritual Freedom, Mahanta Transcripts, Book 17

Sri Harold's wisdom and heart-opening stories of everyday people having extraordinary experiences tell of a secret truth at work in *your* life—there is divine purpose and meaning to every experience you have.

How to Survive Spiritually in Our Times, Mahanta Transcripts, Book 16

Discover how to reinvent yourself spiritually—to thrive in a changing world. Stories, tools, techniques, and spiritual insights to apply in your life now.

Autobiography of a Modern Prophet

This riveting story of Harold Klemp's climb up the Mountain of God will help you discover the keys to your own spiritual greatness.

Those Wonderful ECK Masters

Would you like to have *personal* experience with spiritual masters that people all over the world—since the beginning of time—have looked to for guidance, protection, and divine love? This book includes real-life stories and spiritual exercises to meet eleven ECK Masters.

The Spiritual Laws of Life

Learn how to keep in tune with your true spiritual nature. Spiritual laws reveal the behind-the-scenes forces at work in your daily life.

Available at bookstores, from online booksellers, or directly from Eckankar: www.ECKBooks.org; (952) 380-2200; ECKANKAR, Dept. BK129, PO Box 2000, Chanhassen, MN 55317-2000 USA.

Glossary

Words set in SMALL CAPS are defined elsewhere in this glossary.

Blue Light How the MAHANTA often appears in the inner worlds to the CHELA or seeker.

chela A spiritual student. Often a member of ECKANKAR.

ECK The Life Force, the Holy Spirit, or Audible Life Current which sustains all life.

Eckankar *EHK-ahn-kahr* Religion of the Light and Sound of God. Also known as the Ancient Science of SOUL TRAVEL. A truly spiritual religion for the individual in modern times. The teachings provide a framework for anyone to explore their own spiritual experiences. Established by PAUL TWITCHELL, the modern-day founder, in 1965. The word means Co-worker with God.

ECK Masters Spiritual Masters who can assist and protect people in their spiritual studies and travels. The ECK Masters are from a long line of God-Realized SOULS who know the responsibility that goes with spiritual freedom.

God-Realization The state of God Consciousness. Complete and conscious awareness of God.

HU *HYOO* The most ancient, secret name for God. The singing of the word *HU* is considered a love song to God. It can be sung aloud or silently to oneself to align with God's love.

Karma, Law of The Law of Cause and Effect, action and reaction, justice, retribution, and reward, which applies to the lower or psychic worlds: the Physical, Astral, Causal, Mental, and Etheric PLANES.

Klemp, Harold The present MAHANTA, the LIVING ECK MASTER. SRI Harold Klemp became the Mahanta, the Living ECK Master in 1981. His spiritual name is WAH Z.

Living ECK Master The spiritual leader of ECKANKAR. He leads SOUL back to God. He teaches in the physical world as the Outer Master, in the dream state as the Dream Master, and in the spiritual worlds as the Inner Master. SRI HAROLD KLEMP became the MAHANTA, the Living ECK Master in 1981.

Mahanta An expression of the Spirit of God that is always with you. Sometimes seen as a BLUE LIGHT or Blue Star or in the form of the Mahanta, the LIVING ECK MASTER. The highest state of God Consciousness on earth, only embodied in the Living ECK Master. He is the Living Word.

planes The levels of existence, such as the Physical, Astral, Causal, Mental, Etheric, and SOUL Planes.

Self-Realization Soul recognition. The entering of Soul into the Soul Plane and there beholding Itself as pure Spirit. A state of seeing, knowing, and being.

Shariyat-Ki-Sugmad The sacred scriptures of Eckankar. The scriptures are comprised of twelve volumes in the spiritual worlds. The first two were transcribed from the inner planes by Paul Twitchell, modern-day founder of Eckankar.

Soul The True Self, an individual, eternal spark of God. The inner, most sacred part of each person. Soul can see, know, and perceive all things. It is the creative center of Its own world.

Soul Travel The expansion of consciousness. The ability of Soul to transcend the physical body and travel into the spiritual worlds of God. Soul Travel is taught only by the Living ECK Master. It helps people unfold spiritually and can provide proof of the existence of God and life after death.

Sound and Light of ECK The Holy Spirit. The two aspects through which God appears in the lower worlds. People can experience them by looking and listening within themselves and through Soul Travel.

Spiritual Exercises of ECK Daily practices for direct, personal experiences with the Sound Current. Creative techniques using contemplation and the singing of sacred words to bring the higher awareness of Soul into daily life.

Sri *SREE* A title of spiritual respect, similar to reverend or pastor, used for those who have attained the Kingdom of God. In ECKANKAR, it is reserved for the MAHANTA, the LIVING ECK MASTER.

Sugmad *SOOG-mahd* A sacred name for God. It is the source of all life, neither male nor female, the Ocean of Love and Mercy.

Temples of Golden Wisdom These Golden Wisdom Temples are spiritual temples which exist on the various PLANES—from the Physical to the Anami Lok; CHELAS of ECKANKAR are taken to the temples in the SOUL body to be educated in divine knowledge; sections of the SHARIYAT-KI-SUGMAD, the sacred teachings of ECK, are kept at these temples.

Twitchell, Paul An American ECK MASTER who brought the modern teachings of ECKANKAR to the world through his writings and lectures. His spiritual name is Peddar Zaskq.

Wah Z *WAH zee* The spiritual name of SRI HAROLD KLEMP. It means the secret doctrine. It is his name in the spiritual worlds.

For more explanations of ECKANKAR terms, see *A Cosmic Sea of Words: The ECKANKAR Lexicon* by Harold Klemp.

About the Author

Author Harold Klemp is known as a pioneer of today's focus on "everyday spirituality." He was raised on a Wisconsin farm and attended divinity school. He also served in the US Air Force.

In 1981, after lifetimes of training, he became the spiritual leader of Eckankar, Religion of the Light and Sound of God. His full title is Sri Harold Klemp, the Mahanta, the Living ECK Master. His mission is to help people find their way back to God in this life.

Each year, Harold Klemp speaks to many thousands of seekers at Eckankar seminars. Author of more than one hundred books, he continues to write, including many articles and spiritual-study discourses. His inspiring and practical approach to spirituality helps many thousands of people worldwide find greater freedom, wisdom, and love in their lives.